Juke'n The Uke
Blues, Ragtime & Hokum for 'Ukulele
by Mark Kailana Nelson

CD sold separately.
Additional musical examples available for download at www.mark-o.com

ISBN-013: 978-1477584323
ISBN-10: 1477584323
© 2012 Acme Arts • PO Box 967 • Jacksonville OR 97530.

"The blues is when you drop your bread on the floor and it lands jelly side down."
Leroy "Lefty" Bates

Table of Contents

How This Book Is Organized

The twenty one-songs are arranged more or less in ascending order of difficulty. If you start at the beginning and work your way to the back you will gain a thorough understanding of playing classic blues, hokum and ragtime on your uke.

Of course, if you are the adventurous type—and what 'ukulele player isn't?—just dive in.

For those of you unfamiliar with playing melody on the uke, be sure to see the Fingerpicking Basics lesson on page 10. I've also included a chart of common chord inversions on page 90; refer to this if you need help figuring out some of the fingerings I used.

The first few arrangements of country blues songs are not too challenging. To help you get the feel of it, I've included chord diagrams, playing notes and some fingering hints.

Next come arrangements that show some of the variety of the blues form, followed by more difficult songs transcribed from classic players like Blind Blake, Etta Baker, Big Bill Broonzy, and more. The last few rags ought to give even experienced players a run for their money.

Along the way I've included short lessons on the 12 bar blues form, playing bottleneck style uke, blues notes and blues scales, transposing, and more.

To the best of my knowledge, all of these songs are firmly in the public domain. The arrangements in this book are my own work and are © 2012 acme arts. Feel free to share your playing with your friends, but please do not duplicate the music without permission.

Who This Book Is For

If you love your 'ukulele, can play chords in the first position and want to put a little of that funky stuff into your playing, this book is for you. That is not to say it won't be a bit of a challenge; some of these arrangements require deft fingerwork all the way up the neck, while others will be in the reach of almost any intermediate player.

If you are unfamiliar with playing fingerstyle 'ukulele, I strongly recommend that you pick up my book entitled— what else?—*Learn to Play Fingerstyle Solos For 'Ukulele* (Mel Bay Publications).

Although all of the arrangements can be played on any 'ukulele in standard tuning, most sound better played on an instrument with a low G string. You can pick up low G uke strings from most music stores or online retailers; in a pinch take a classical guitar G string and cut it down. You might have to modify your nut and bridge to accommodate the wider string. Yet another good reason to invest in another uke!

Like many players, I prefer the longer scale and fuller sound of a tenor 'ukulele.

A word about Baritone 'Ukulele:

Baritone ukers can play along, too. Just play the TAB as written, and you'll be fine. I've included a section on how to transpose the chords on page 93 so you'll know where you are in the musical universe.

TAB and Musical Notation

All of the music is written in standard notation and Tablature for 'ukulele.

Tablature, or TAB, is an ancient system of musical notation in which lines represent the instrument's strings.

Fingering positions are indicated by numbers. TAB doesn't give any indication of how long to hold each note; for that refer to the staff above the TAB. (If you are unfamiliar with standard musical notation, keep reading.)

Note that the strings are numbered starting with the string closest to the floor, so A is the first string, E the second, C the third and G the fourth. As you can see from the example below, TAB reverses the apparent order of the strings.

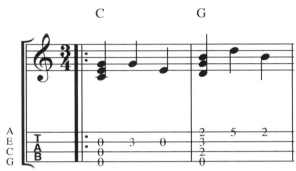

In this example play the open second, third and fourth strings on beat one. Then fret the second string on the third fret followed by the open second string. In the second measure, start with a G chord, then reach up to the fifth fret on the first string and finish back at the second fret, first string.

Picking hand fingerings have not been indicated: experiment with different combinations to see what works best for you.

For arrangements with an alternating bass pattern, I play both the third and fourth strings (and sometimes the second) with my thumb.

Here are some more TAB symbols and playing techniques you will encounter.

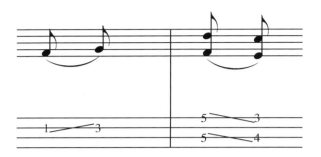

Slide: Pick the first note—or notes—and then slide up or down to the second. Be sure to give each note its full time value!

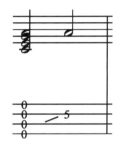

When playing bottleneck style, you often slide into a note from an indeterminate position a few frets below.

Hammer-on: Play the first note, then rapidly press your finger down to the fretboard to sound the second note.

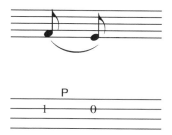

Pull-off: Play the first note, then quickly pull off your finger to sound the lower note.

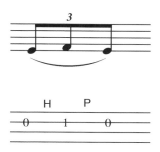

Hammer/pull combination: A rapid combination of a hammer-on and pull-off executed as a quick flick of the finger.

You can often tell how to finger a given measure by looking ahead and "collapsing" the individual notes into chords or double stops.
For instance, this:

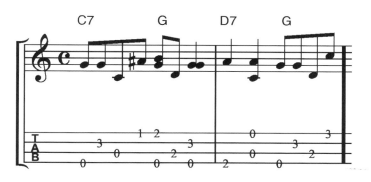

is played out of these positions:

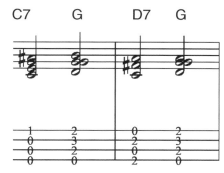

Although it is not necessary to know how to read musical notation to play the songs in this book, knowledge of a few musical symbols will greatly enhance your enjoyment.

Since the TAB will give you the correct pitches on a properly tuned instrument, you really only have to worry about the rhythm of a particular piece.

Music is divided into **measures**, each of which contains the number of beats delineated by the **time signature:**

 4/4 means four beats per measure, each quarter note counts as one beat.

 3/4 is three beats per measure, each quarter note counts as one beat.

Occasionally alternate symbols are used for the time signature. **Common Time** ![Common Time symbol] is the same as 4/4.

Each beat can be further divided into smaller and smaller units:

𝅝 The longest note is the whole note; it is the equivalent of four quarter notes, or four counts.

𝅗𝅥 The half note is equal to two quarter notes.

𝅘𝅥 The quarter note gets one count.

𝅘𝅥𝅮 Two eighth notes equals a quarter note.

𝅘𝅥𝅯 The sixteenth note is half as long as the eighth note; so two sixteenths equal one eighth, four sixteenths equal a quarter, and sixteen equal a whole note.

Rests correspond to each of the different note values.

𝅝 = ▬   𝅗𝅥 = ▬   𝅘𝅥 = 𝄽   𝅘𝅥𝅮 = 𝄾   𝅘𝅥𝅯 = 𝄿

A dot placed next to a note (or rest) lengthens it by one half of its value. For example:

𝅘𝅥. = 𝅘𝅥𝅮 𝅘𝅥𝅮 𝅘𝅥𝅮

Ties are used for notes that are held for their combined values.

𝅘𝅥𝅮 ‿ 𝅘𝅥 This figure would be held as long as three eighth notes.

Triplets are groups of three notes that are played in the space of two.

For example, three eighth note triplets

would be played in the same amount of time as two eighth notes.

Blues and ragtime share a ragged, syncopated rhythm that swings. Swing is hard to describe, but easy to recognize. So when you see this: play something like this: ♪. ♪♪. ♪

As the master said, "It don't mean a thing if it ain't got that swing!"

‖: :‖	**Repeat signs**: repeat the enclosed phrase one time before going on to the next one.
1 ⌐———————⌐ :‖	This sign means play the measures under the sign on the first time through and then go back to the beginning of the section. On the repeat you skip over the first ending and play the second ending.
D.C.	From the Italian, **Da Capo**, meaning "Head." This sign directs you to go back to the beginning of the music. **D.C. al Fine** directs you to play from the beginning to the designated end of the song.
D.S.	**Dal Segno**, or "to the sign," tells you to look for the symbol (𝄋) and play that section next rather than returning to the beginning. **D.S. al Coda** means play from the sign to the coda sign, then jump to the coda.
⊕	A **Coda** sign is often used to mark the ending of the piece. When you see *To Coda*, skip down to the section with the coda sign to finish the song. Coda is Italian for "Tail," by the way.
rit.	Also **Ritard.** Gradually slow the pace to bring the music to a graceful conclusion.

Blues You Can Use
Fingerpicking Basics

With the exception of "That Lonesome Train That Took My Baby Away," all of the songs in this book require a great deal of independence of your thumb and fingers. If you have already mastered this style, feel free to skip ahead. If not, some time spent on this technique will pay great dividends later.

There are as many ways to approach fingerpicking as there are players. That's why I wrote the book *Learn to Play Fingerstyle Solos for 'Ukulele* (Mel Bay Publications). You'll find graded lessons and a collection of songs in many different styles, including blues and ragtime, that will set you firmly on the path.

That being said, here's a little tune to get you picking right away.

The nursery rhyme "Brother John" is a dandy vehicle for teaching your thumb and fingers to dance. In just a few short bars, you encounter many essential fingerpicking techniques.

Before you tackle the 2nd half of the arrangement, play through the melody with the chords a few times to get the feel of it. Notice that the tune consists of four short musical phases and that each phrase consists of a single bar that repeats.

Let's get started. **Warning**: Don't just dive in and play the song from top to bottom. If you do, you might make mistakes and risk teaching yourself to play it wrong. The trick is to take it slowly, repeating one phrase at a time until your hands have had time to develop muscle memory. Tedious? You bet, but I'm afraid that there is no short cut.

Measures 9 & 10: Play each of the double stops (note pairs that sound at the same time) as a pinch, using your thumb for the notes on the 4th and 3rd strings, your index finger on the 2nd string and your middle finger on the 1st. Take it as slowly as you need to in order to keep a steady beat without making a mistake.

Measures 11 & 12: Same idea. Note the chord change at beat 3 and the extra "bass" note played with your thumb on beat 4. (Note: like most of the arrangements in this book, this sounds better with a low G string on your uke.)

Measures 13 & 14: Notice that notes on the downbeats are played as pinches while the others sound in between the beats.

Play the first beat as a pinch on strings 1 and 4, followed by a quick flick up to the 5th fret. Beat two is another pinch on strings 1 and 3, followed by a single note at the first fret. I alternate between my index and middle fingers for these eighth notes. Now you know why I said to take it slow.

Change to an F chord on beat 3; the double stops on beats 3 and 4 are both thumb-finger pinches.

Measures 15 & 16: No surprises here.

Once you can play "Brother John" at a nice steady tempo, you'll be ready to tackle the songs in the next part of the book.

Brother John

Fingerpicking excercise

trad

Standard tuning
Basic Melody with Chords

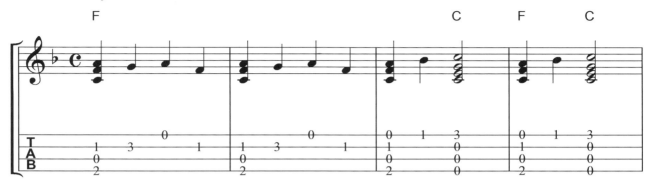

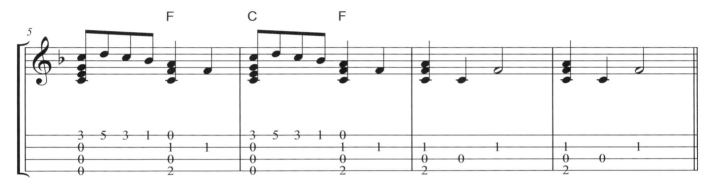

Fingerpicked

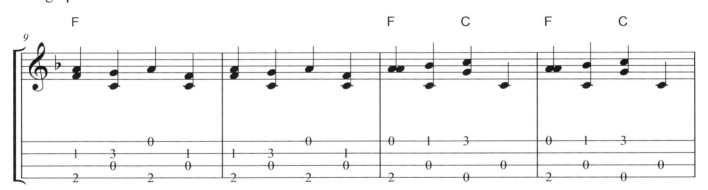

"The blues is the roots, the rest is the fruits."

Willie Dixon

Goin' Up The Country

I looked down the river about one o'clock
I saw a big catfish swimming' around
I got so hungry didn't know what to do,
I'm gonna get me a catfish, too.

Country blues pickers often employ a steady alternating bass on the lowest strings while playing syncopated melodies on top. With strong melodies and a verse/chorus structure, these songs are more like 19th Century folk and popular song styles than the call-and-response form more often associated with the blues. In fact, many early country blues artists were called "songsters" by their contemporaries. Often associated with the Piedmont region of the Southeastern US, you can find great country blues artists in the Delta and Texas, too.

The next five songs will get you playing country blues on your uke.

To help you with the fingering, I've included fretboard diagrams and notes for the first few songs.

Richland Woman Blues
from Mississippi John Hurt

Mississippi John Hurt's gentle voice and easy-going guitar style mesmerized audiences twice; once in the 1920s, when his first recordings were made, and again after his rediscovery during the folk music boom of the 60s.

"Richland Woman Blues" is rightfully one of his most famous songs. No one is really sure where it came from; it is possible he adapted a now-forgotten song from the early years of the last century.

Measures 1 & 2: Hold down an F chord for the first measure, and change to a Bb in Measure 2, even when you are only playing single notes. Use your pinky to grab that blue note on the 4th fret. Remember to play the bass notes on strings 4 & 3 with your thumb; a steady alternating bass is the hallmark of this style.

Here's what the fingering looks like for measures 1 & 2:

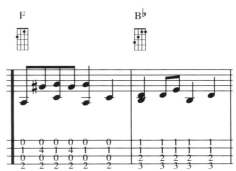

Measure 3: While holding a Bb chord, relax your barre so that the first string can sound an open note. Use your pinky as before to reach the note on the fourth string.

Measures 8 & 9: As before, hold an F chord for both measures. From here on out it ought to be smooth sailing

Richland Woman Blues

Give me red lipstick and a bright purple rouge
A shingle bob haircut and a shot of good booze
Hurry down, sweet daddy, come blow' your horn
If you come too late, your mama will be gone

Come along young man, everything is settin' right
My husband's gone away till next Saturday night
Hurry down, sweet daddy, come blow' your horn
If you come too late, your mama will be gone

Now, I'm raring to go, got red shoes on my feet
My mind is sittin' right for a Tin Lizzie seat

The red rooster said, "Cockle-doodle-do-do"
Richland woman says, "Any dude will do"

With my rosy red garters, pink hose on my feet
Turkey red bloomers, they got a rumble seat

Every Sunday mornin', church people watch me go
My wings have sprouted out – preacher told me so

Dress skirt cut high, then they cut low
Don't think I'm a sport, keep on watchin' me go
Hurry down, sweet daddy, come blow' your horn
If you come too late, your mama will be gone

Fishin' Blues

from Henry Thomas

Low G tuning

16

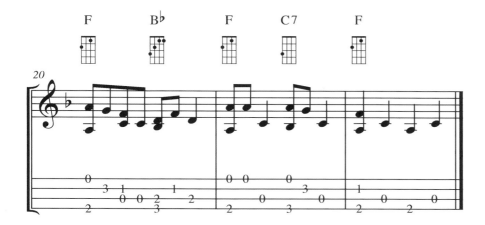

This delightful song first came to the attention of the wider world in 1952 as the closer to Henry Smith's monumental–and eccentric–"Anthology of American Folk Music." Born in 1874 in Big Sandy Texas, Henry "Ragtime Texas" Thomas remains an important bridge between 19th and early 20th Century folk music styles. On the original "Fishin' Blues" recorded in 1927, Thomas accompanied himself on guitar and quills–a type of pan pipe.

Measures 1 - 4: Hold down an F chord for the first three measures, even when you are only playing single notes. Use your pinky to grab that note on the 4th fret.

Here's what the fingering looks like for measures 1 & 2:

These first four measures are the verse. Note that the third verse is shorter, so you don't play the repeats.

Fishin' Blues

Went up the hill about 12 o'clock
Reached right back and got me a pole
Went to the hardware and got me a hook
Put that hook on the end of my line

chorus
Said you been fishin' all of the time, I'm a going fishin' too
You can bet your life, your sweet wife
Is goin' to catch more fish than you
Any fish'll bite if you got good bait,
Now here's a little something I'd like to relate
Any fish'll bite if you got good bait,
I'm a goin' fishin', yes I'm goin' fishin'
And my baby's goin' fishin', too

I looked down the river about one o'clock
I saw a big catfish swimming' around
I got so hungry didn't know what to do,
I'm gonna get me a catfish, too.

Put on your skillet, put on the lead
Goin' to cook up some shortenin' bread

Staggerlee
from Mississippi John Hurt

trad

19

Based on the 1895 murder of William Lyons by "Stag" (or "Stagger") Lee Shelton in St. Louis, there are probably as many versions of this classic ballad as there are singers. I took my lyrics from several sources; the uke part draws heavily on the masterful guitar playing of Mississippi John Hurt.

I chose to create a slightly different arrangement for the instrumental and vocal parts of the song just to create a little variety. After you become familiar with each, feel free to mix and match licks.

Measures 1-4: Play all of these out of a 1st position G chord. The syncopation might take a little getting used to, so take it slow. Once you have mastered these four measures, the remainder of the arrangement will be a piece of cake.

Notice that the song has an unusual 11 measure form.

Measure 12-15: For the vocal, the picking is a little more straight forward. The rest of the arrangement is essentially the same as the first 11 bars.

I generally let my mood dictate how many verses I sing before playing an instrumental chorus.

Staggerlee

Could've been a Saturday evening, could've been a Saturday night,
Staggerlee and Billy D. Lyon got in a great big fight
He is a bad man, old cruel Staggerlee

Police man tell me, how can it be,
You can arrest everybody, 'cept old Staggerlee?
He is a bad man, old cruel Staggerlee

"Staggerlee,' said Billy D. Lyon, "please don't take my life,
I've got two little children and a loving wife"

"I don't care about your children, I don't care about your wife.
You took my Stetson hat now I'm bound to take your life"

Last time I saw Billy D. Lyon he was lyin' on the floor
Staggerlee, he shot him, with a pearl handled forty-four

Gentlemen of the jury, what do you think of that?
Staggerlee shot Billy D. Lyon 'bout a five dollar Stetson hat

Gentlemen of the jury, raise up your right hand,
At five o'clock they hung him, that was the end of that bad man
Talkin' 'bout that bad man, old cruel Staggerlee

Could've been a Saturday evening, could've been a Saturday night,
Staggerlee and Billy D. Lyon got in a great big fight
He is a bad man, old cruel Staggerlee

"So the blues player, he ain't worried and bothered, but he's got something for the worried people."

Roosevelt Sykes

Let the Mermaids Flirt With Me

from Mississippi John Hurt

trad

Low G tuning

Here's another gem from Mississippi John Hurt. His guitar playing and sweet tempered singing influenced several generations. I started out playing John Hurt's stuff on the guitar when I was in my teens, so it is only natural I'd adapt his style to the uke. But don't be fooled, although his playing seems simple, close listening reveals tremendous depth.

Like many John Hurt songs, this one is an echo of an earlier time.

Let the Mermaids Flirt With Me

Blues all on the ocean, blues all in the air
I can't stay here no longer, I've got no steamship fare,
When my earthly trials are over, cast my body out in the sea,
Save on the undertaker's bills, let the mermaids flirt with me

I do not work for pleasure, earthly treasure I'll know no more
The only reason I that work at all is to keep the wolf from my door
When my earthly trials are over, cast my body out in the sea,
Save on the undertaker's bills, let the mermaids flirt with me

My wife controls our happy home, my sweetheart I can't find
The only thing I can call my own is a worried and a troubled mind
When my earthly trials are over, cast my body out in the sea,
Save on the undertaker's bills, let the mermaids flirt with me

There's blues all in my body, my sweetheart has forsaken me
If I ever want see her face again, I'll have to swim across the sea
When my earthly trials are over, cast my body out in the sea,
Save on the undertaker's bills, let the mermaids flirt with me

Moving Day

trad

24

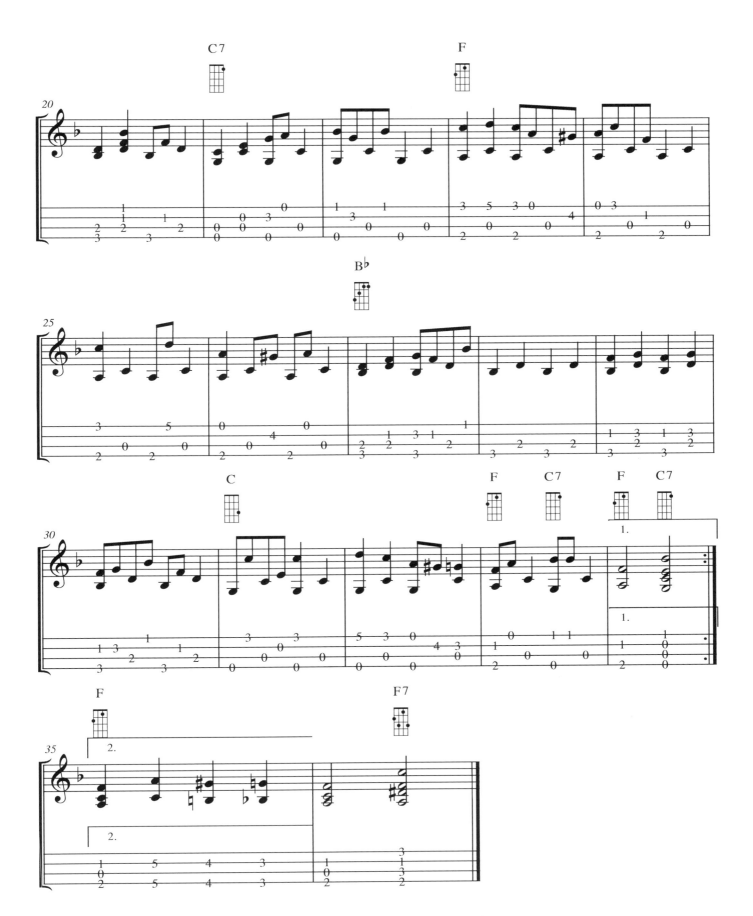

25

Though Andrew Sterling and Harry Von Tilzer wrote the original "Moving Day" in 1906, most people know it from Charlie Poole and the North Carolina Rambler's recording from the late 20s or early 30s. However, this version differs from either of those sources.

I originally learned it sometime in the mid 1960s, most likely off of a Jim Kweskin LP. I recorded the 'ukulele arrangement found here on my 2009 CD "Funtime Uke-A-Rama."

Moving Day

Landlord says this morning to me
"Give me your key, this place ain't free
I can't get no rent out of you
Pack up your things and skidoo."
"I'm just waiting for my Bill to come home
He's my honey from the honeycomb
He'll have money 'cause he told me so this morning"

chorus
Because it's moving day, moving day
Rip the carpet up off the floor
Pick up your overcoat and get out the door
Because it's moving day
Pack up your bags and get away
If you can't pay the rent you can live out in a tent
It's moo-oo-oo-ving, whoa it's moving day

Bill comes in all covered with snow
I say, "Hello, give me some dough.
Here's the landlord looking for rent."
And Bill says, "I ain't got a cent."
We'll be leaving just as quick as we can,
You can try and catch us Mister Landlord Man
We'll be heading back to Dixieland this morning

Good Mornin', Blues

Good mornin, blues, blues how do you do?
Good mornin, blues, blues how do you do?
I feel mighty bad this mornin', because I can't get along with you

Some say the blues are America's oldest and most enduring musical contribution to the world. Some say the blues came from Africa, some say the blues started in the fields during slavery days, some say singing the blues are the only way to get rid of the blues.

The name mostly likely comes from the "blue devils," an old term for that lowdown dirty feeling we all get from time to time. Although the form is undoubtably older, the first 12 bar blues, "Dallas Blues" by Hart Wand, was published in 1912.

One thing is certain: some day, some time, everybody gets the blues.

Blues in the Bottle
from Prince Albert Hunt

trad

Seems like everybody has tried their hand at this one over the years. The original 1928 recording by Prince Albert Hunt's Texas Ramblers is considered to be one of the earliest examples of the hot fiddle-based musical style that gave birth to Western Swing.

The original recording is quirky to say the least; I doubt that any two verses share the same number of measures, or even the same number of beats per measure! Somewhere along the line someone regularized the chord progression to a standard 12 bar blues.

Note that sometimes the bass changes from an alternating pattern to a steady drone on the G string, as in measure 9.

I seldom play two verses the same way. Measures 8 & 9, 10 & 11 and 12 & 13 are good candidates for improvisation.

Blues in the Bottle

Blues in the bottle, blues in the bottle
The stopper's in my hand, pretty mama
Blues in the bottle, the stopper's in my hand
I'm going back to Fort Worth because you found another man

Go dig you taters, go dig your taters, its tater digging time, pretty mama
Go dig your taters, its tater digging time
Old man Jack Frost, he's gone and killed your vine

I asked my baby, I asked my baby, could she stand to see me cry, pretty mama
I asked my baby, could she stand to see me cry
She said, "Whoa now, daddy, I could stand to see you die!"

Rooster chews tobacco, rooster chews tobacco and the hen uses snuff, pretty mama
Rooster chews tobacco and the hen uses snuff
The little chickens don't use nothing, they just strut their stuff

I'm goin' to Chattanoogie, goin' to Chattanoogie, just to see the ponies run, pretty mama
Goin' to Chattanoogie just to see the ponies run
And if I win some money I'm goin' to give you some

Blues in the bottle, blues in the bottle
The stopper's in my hand, pretty mama
Blues in the bottle, the stopper's in my hand
I'm lookin' for a woman, who's lookin' for a man

Blues You Can Use
12 Bars and the Truth

Almost everyone has heard the term "12 bar blues," but what does it mean, really? Are the blues a lyrical style, an emotional feeling, a type of scale, a chord progression, or a musical style?

The short answer is: the blues are all that, and more.

One common feature of the blues is a three line lyrical style, with the first line is repeated twice.

> I'm goin' up the country, in the rain and snow
> I'm goin' up the country, in the rain and snow
> When I'll be back, honey, I just don't know

Supporting this is a 12 measure long progression based on the tonic, subdominant, and dominant chords. Hence the name "12 bar blues." The form is so common that, no matter where you go, play a blues and musicians you've never met can instantly join in.

Although it comes in a number of variations, at its most basic a 12 bar blues in the key of A looks like this:

A	A	A	A
D	D	A	A
E	D	A	A

Notice that in the key of A, the tonic chord (A) is built on the 1st note of the scale and the subdominant chord (D) is derived from the 4th scale degree (counting the notes, you get A-B-C-D, or 1-2-3-4). The dominant chord, E7, is based on the 5th scale tone (A-B-C-D-E). Musicians often use Roman numerals to indicate chords, so this same 12 bar blues in A could be written like this, where the A chord is I; the D chord IV, and the E chord the V:

I	I	I	I
IV	IV	I	I
V	IV	I	I

Remember the three line lyrical form? Here's how it works: Each line corresponds to four bars of the blues progression. So the first line is sung over the I chord; it is repeated over the IV chord; and "answered" in the final four bars. Often the vocal line is followed by a short instrumental phrase in call and response fashion.

When you play a 12 bar blues, it sometimes sounds better to use dominant 7th chords for the I and the IV to help move things along. The last 2 bars often have an instrumental lick called a turnaround to bring things back to the beginning.

Here's is another typical 12 bar blues progression. Notice that the last measure has two beats on the I chord, followed by two beats on the V7.

I	IV	I	I7
IV	IV	I	I7
V7	IV7	I	I - V7

So what's with the Roman numerals? If you start thinking about chords in terms of their numerical relationship to the key of the song, it gets very easy to transpose. (See page 92 for more information about transposing.)

Here's how it works: in the key of C, the tonic, or I chord, would naturally be C. Counting four scale degrees up from C gives you F (C-D-E-F); so the IV, or subdominant chord is F, and the dominant, or IV is built on the next scale tone, G (C-D-E-F-G).

C	F	C	C7
F	F	C	C7
G7	F7	C	C - G7

Taking the key of F, you get:

F	Bb	F	F7
Bb	Bb	F	F7
C7	Bb7	F	F - C7

Practise transposing to other keys, too. You will find that becomes second nature after a while.

Many songs in this book, including, "Blues in the Bottle," "Hey Hey," "Tell Me Baby" and the first section of "Palakiko Blues" are based on 12 bar blues.

"Wild Cow Blues" is mostly a straight ahead 12 bar blues, but it extends the form for one of the verses. "That Lonesome Train That Took My Baby Away" drops one measure to become an 11 bar blues!

There are other standard blues forms, too. "K.C. Moan Blues" and "Guitar Rag" are types of 16 bar blues. You'll also encounter 8 and 10 bar blues. Some songs, like "Okolehau Blues," don't seem to fit in any bag.

But far and away the 12 bar blues reigns supreme. Master it and you will be on your way to playing literally thousands of classic blues, swing, and rock songs. And that's the truth!

Wild Cow Blues

trad

Low G tuning

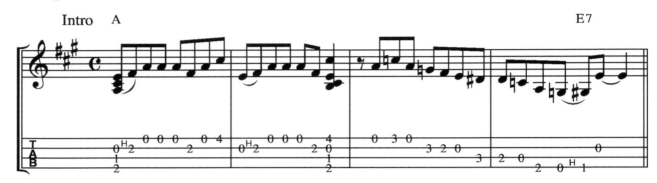

Verse

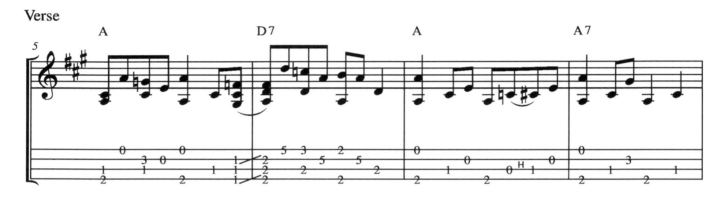

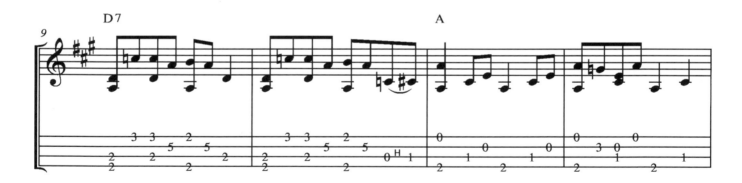

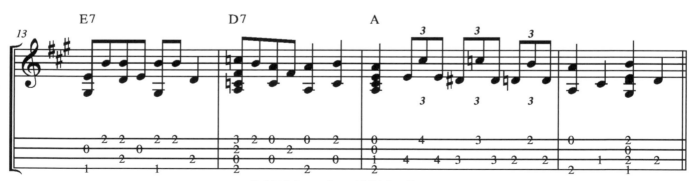

Solo 1

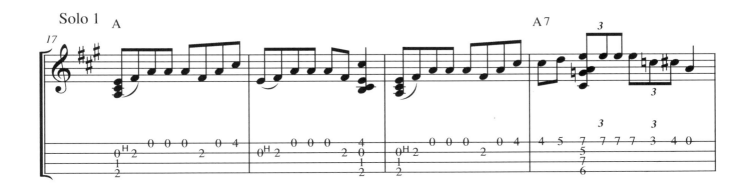

Solo 2

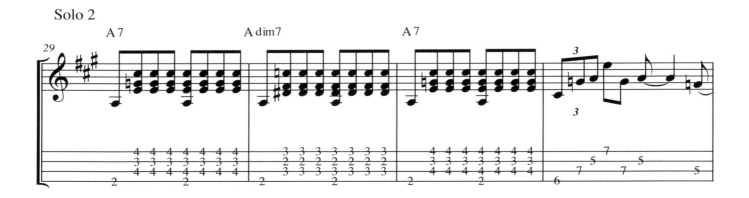

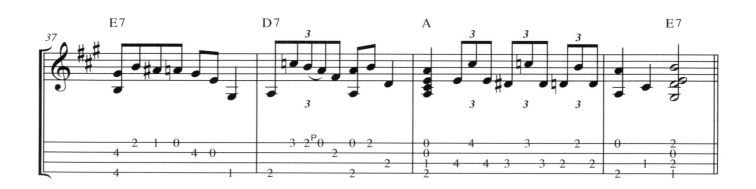

Kokomo Arnold's 1934 recording of "Milk Cow Blues" spawned an entire musical genre. Subsequent artists recording the song include Robert Johnson (as "Milk Cow's Calf Blues"), Big Joe William's "Wild Cow Blues," Bob Wills and His Texas Playboys (twice, once as "Milk Cow Blues," and again, with slightly different lyrics, as "Brain Cloudy Blues"), Elvis Presley, Willie Nelson and even Aerosmith.

Just for fun, I arranged it as it might have been played by the Wills Band... assuming Bob played the ukulele, of course. The lyrics come from all over the place.

The tab consists of 4 parts: an introduction, a typical verse, and two solos. On the recording, the solos follow the third verse, feel free to insert them anywhere the fancy strikes you.

For verses 4 and 5, marked "Stop verse" on the lyrics, strum an A chord for the first four measures— or 8 measures for verse 5—and then continue with the verse on the IV chord.

Wild Cow Blues

Good morning, I said blues how do you do?
Good morning, I said blues how do you do?
I feel mighty bad this morning, because I can't get along with you.

I cannot do right baby, when you won't do right yourself
I cannot do right baby, when you won't do right yourself
I'll be your lowdown dog, but please don't dog me around

Stop verse
It takes a rocking chair to rock, a rubber ball to roll,
Takes a lot of loving just to pacify my soul
Lord I don't feel welcome, anywhere I go
Because that woman I've been lovin' has sent me from her door

Stop verse
Now you can read out your hymn book, preach out your bible, too
Fall down on your knees and let the good lord help you, too
I'm going to stop crying going to leave you alone
If you don't think I'm leaving you can count the days I'm gone
'Cause you're gonna need, your gonna need my help some day,
If you can't quit your sinning, please quit your lowdown ways.

I woke up this morning, I looked down the road
I believe I heard my wild cow, mama, when she began to low
If you see my wild cow please send her home
'Cause I ain't had no milk and butter, since my wild cow's been gone

K.C. Moan Blues
from The Memphis Jug Band

trad

Low G Tuning

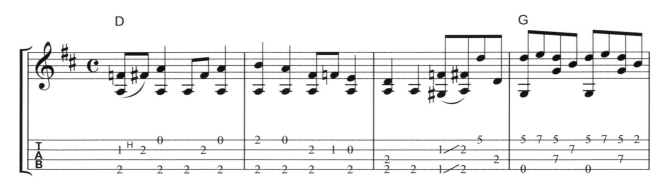

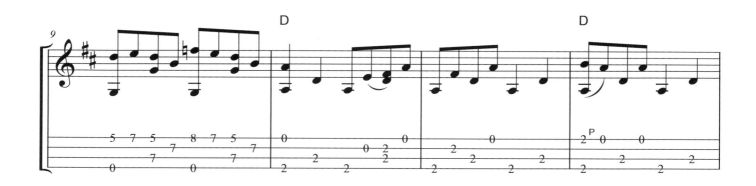

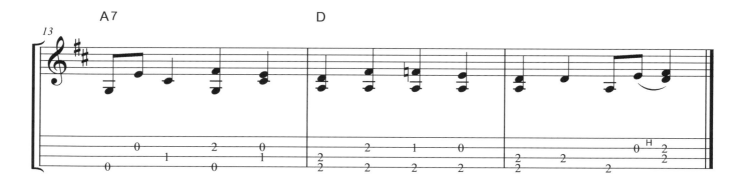

36

A standard of both the blues and jug band repertoire. I cobbled together this version from a couple of different sources, notably early recordings of the Memphis Jug Band and Andrew and Jim Baxter. The song goes by a number of different names, including "K.C. Railroad Blues," "K.C. Blues," and "K.C. Moan."

As you can see, this is a 16 bar blues. Although not quite as common as 12 bar blues, various 16 bar forms show up in blues and jazz.

Measures 1-3: Play these with a steady monotonic bass on the 4th string. Though it is not notated, I hold down a D chord throughout.

Note the slide in Measure 3; just move everything back one fret and slide the whole chord. Then reach up with your pinky for the high D at the 5th fret.

Measures 4 & 5: Hold an inversion of the G at the 5th fret, with the lowest string open and switch to an alternating bass pattern.

Measure 6 & 7 are played out of a D chord barred at the 5th fret.

K.C Moan Blues

I thought I heard that K.C. when she blows
Oh, I thought I heard that K.C. when she blows
I thought I heard that K.C. when she blows
She blows just like my woman is aboard

When I get back on that K.C. road (3x)
Gonna love my baby like I never loved before

There's comin' a time when a woman don't need no man (3x)
Then you better watch out when she picks up that frying' pan

(alternative verse)
There's comin' a time when a woman don't need no man (3x)
Honey I love you, God knows I do

Hello Central, get me that long distance line (3X)
I just want to talk to that bride of mine

I thought I heard that K.C. when she moans
Oh, I thought I heard that K.C. when she moans
I thought I heard that K.C. when she moans
She moans just like my woman is aboard

Hey Hey
from Bill Broonzy

trad

Low G tuning

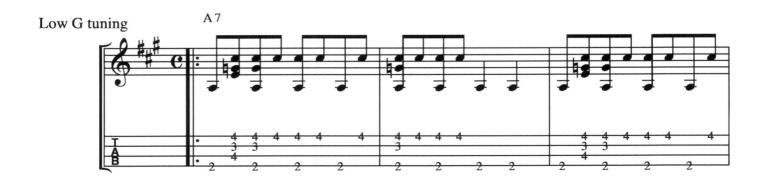

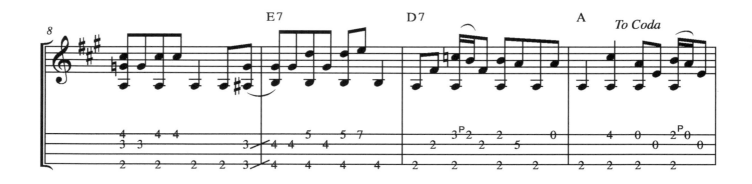

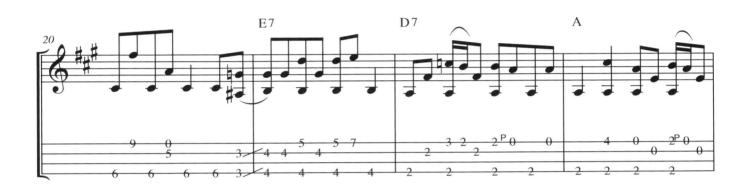

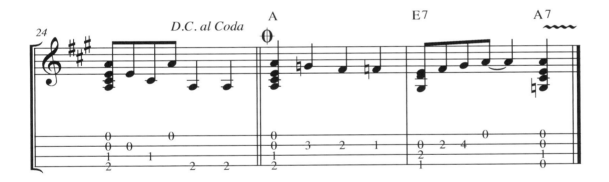

Big Bill Broonzy was born in either 1984 or 1906, did or did not serve in WW I, and may not even have been named Broonzy–biography was not his stong suit. He was a hugely influential singer and guitarist from the 1920s all the way until his death in 1958.

In 1938 Broonzy was selected to replace a recently murdered Robert Johnson at the seminal "From Spirituals to Swing Concert" at Carnegie Hall.

The instrumental "Hey Hey" is based on a swinging instrumental he called "Hey, Hey, Hey." I figured I could get by with one less "Hey" 'cause the uke's so much smaller than the guitar.

Play it with a medium shuffle.

That Lonesome Train That Took My Baby Away
(Jackson Stomp)

trad

from Papa Charlie McCoy

Standard Ukulele Tuning
Plectrum style

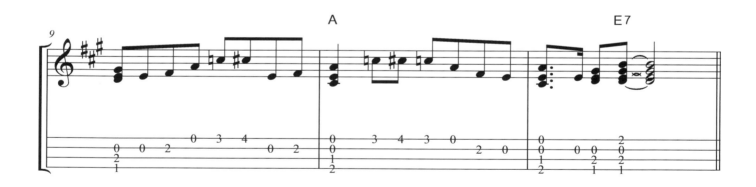

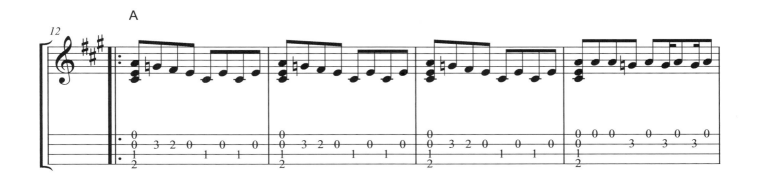

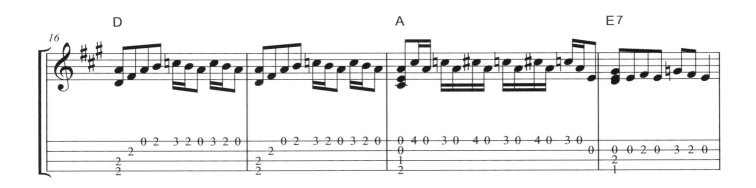

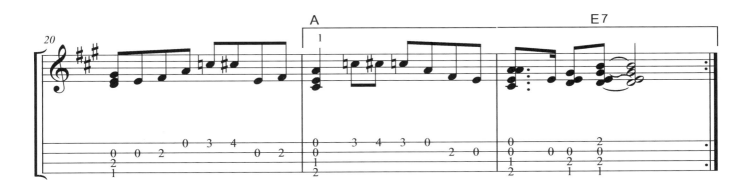

Papa Charlie McCoy recorded this rousing 11 bar blues twice in the mid 1920s; once as an instrumental called "Jackson Stomp" with The Mississippi Mudsteppers, and once as a vocal. Most likely the band on both those sessions included Bo Carter on fiddle. McCoy played the banjo-mandolin and enjoyed a long career as a sideman.

Consider this arrangement a two-few. Play it as an instrumental and call it "Jackson Stomp," or sing it as "That Lonesome Train That Took My Baby Away."

I play this on a uke in standard re-entrant tuning, using a flatpick. On the first part, strum the first chord and then choke it immediately.

If it is too difficult to sing over this melody, just play the chords and use the two parts of the arrangement as instrumental solos.

That Lonesome Train That Took My Baby Away

Woke up this morning, found something wrong
My lovin' baby had took that train and gone
I want you to starch my jumper, wash my overalls
I'm going to ride that train that they call the cannonball

It's just poor agent Closure, poor agent Brown;
That woman I love is fixin' to blow this town
Mean old fireman, that cruel old engineer,
Gonna take my baby and leave me longtime here

It ain't no telling' what that train will do
Take your baby and run right over you,
Now that engineer man I ought teach him myself
Take women from their husbands, baby, that ain't right

I walked down the tracks when the sun was going to shine
Looks like every minute I was going to lose my mind,
My knees were weak, my footsteps was all I heard
Looks like every minute I was stepping in another world.

Woke up this morning, found something wrong
That woman I love had took that train and gone
I want you to starch my jumper, wash my overalls
I'm going to ride that train that they call the cannonball

Blues You Can Use
How to Play Bottleneck Slide Uke

"As I nodded in the railroad station while waiting for a train that had been delayed nine hours, life suddenly took me by the shoulder and awakened me with a start. A lean, loose-jointed Negro had commenced plunking a guitar beside me while I slept. As he played, he pressed a knife on the strings of the guitar in a manner popularized by Hawaiian guitarists who used steel bars. The effect was unforgettable. His song, too, struck me instantly. 'Goin' where the Southern cross the Dog*.'

The singer repeated the line three times, accompanying himself on guitar with the weirdest music I had ever heard."

Composer W.C. Handy reminiscing about the first time he heard the blues, circa 1903.

Green River Blues
Charlie Patton

I see a river rollin' like a log
I wade up Green River, rollin' like a log
I wade up Green River, Lord, rollin' like a log

Think I heard the Marion whistle blow
I dreamed I heard the Marion whistle blow,
And it blew just like my baby gettin' on board

I'm goin' where the Southern cross the Dog
I'm goin' where the Southern cross the Dog
I'm goin' where the Southern cross the Dog

Some people say the Green River blues ain't bad
Some people say the Green River blues ain't bad
Then it must not been the Green River blues I had

* The Southern was a railroad. Another railroad, the Yazoo Delta, was popularly known as the Yellow Dog. The Southern and the Yazoo Delta tracks crossed in Moorhead, Mississippi.

Handy's story is one of the first tantalizing hints of a unique style of music. Although the Hawaiian steel guitar was invented by Joseph Kekuku circa 1890, and Hawaiian musicians and music had taken America by storm in the early decades of the 20th Century, it is unlikely that it had penetrated as far as the Mississippi Delta by 1903. Unlikely, but not impossible. Of course, Handy might also have gotten his dates wrong.

So, did the bottleneck style come from the Hawaiians? Or did African-American guitarists attached to the US army stationed in the newly appropriated Territory of Hawaii bring their slide playing with them and influence the budding Hawaiian musicians? No one knows.

Unlike the Hawaiian steel guitarists, bottleneck slide players usually hold their guitars upright. The slide—which might be a hollow piece of steel, a large socket wrench, or the broken-off neck of a bottle—slips over one of the fingers of the fretting hand, leaving the other fingers to fret notes normally.

These days you don't have to risk life and limb by cracking off the neck of a wine bottle, so head down to the local music store and pick up a comfortable slide or two. I prefer *Gen-U-Wine* glass slides made from a recycled wine bottle by blues musician Rick Park (**www.RickParkArts.com**). Check out his web site for great playing tips, too.

Bottleneck Blues Lesson

"Spanish" Tuning
G-E-C-G
Bottleneck Style

trad

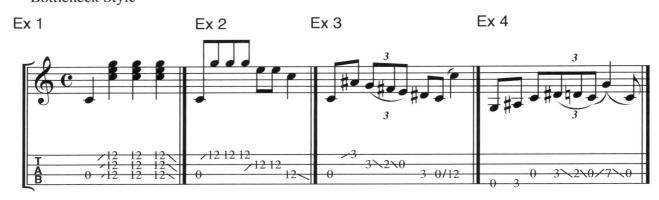

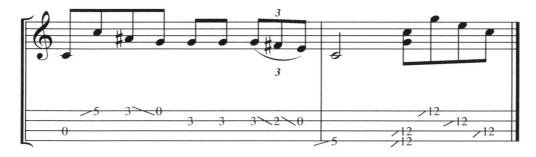

44

Getting Started

Playing slide is not difficult, but it takes some getting used to. Find a comfortable slide and place it over your pinky or ring finger, bending the finger slightly to hold it in place. Some players even use their middle fingers for slide.

Practice running the slide up and down the strings, stopping directly over the fret wire at each fret. Drag one finger along the strings behind the slide to damp the ugly vibrations between the slide and the nut.

Tuning: Slide players most often play in "open" tunings, where the strings are tuned to a full chord. For "Spanish" tuning–named after the popular parlor guitar piece "Spanish Fandango" by Henry Worrall–simply lower the first string a whole step from A to G. Strum all the open strings to sound a C major chord. By the way, if you have my "Learn to Play Slack Key Style 'Ukulele" book, this is the same as "Taropatch" tuning.

"Vastopol"–G-D-B-G–is another common tuning. It, too, takes its name from an old song.

Example 1: After playing the open C string, place the slide a few frets lower than the 12th fret, grab three strings and slide up, be sure to stop exactly above the fret wire, not behind it as you would when fretting the notes. Play the next two notes, then let the slide fall down below the 12th fret.

The trick is to take enough time for the sliding notes to sound like a wailing human voice. Try starting the slide from different places–the 10th fret, or somewhere between the 8th and 9th frets, or the 11th fret. Ditto with the downward slide, let the notes ring, and then slowly move the slide back down the fret board.

Example 2: Same idea. It will take some practice before you can sound the single notes cleanly… but not too cleanly. This is the blues, after all. Dirty is good.

Examples 3 & 4: More single string practice. In Ex 4, practice playing the note at the 3rd fret, 4th string with either your finger or the slide. Once you are comfortable with the first four exercises, try playing through all four measures at a steady tempo.

Example 5: Playing chords in open tunings is a piece of cake: just hold the slide across all of the strings at the 5th fret for an F chord. But slide players rarely play full chords, instead they move around between the 3rd and 5th frets for licks based on the F chord.

After you are comfortable with this exercise, try making up some licks of your own.

Example 6: Same idea, different chord. The chromatic run in the second measure ends on an F natural, the 7th of a G7 chord.

Example 7: Here's a typical ending lick to practice.

Vibrato–a subtle wavering of the pitch–is one of the hardest slide techniques to master. Whenever you stick on a note for awhile, practice moving the slide slightly higher and lower–as much or as little as sounds good to you. Try shaking at different speeds to develop your own signature sound.

Tell Me, Baby

"Spanish" Tuning
G-E-C-G
Bottleneck Style

trad

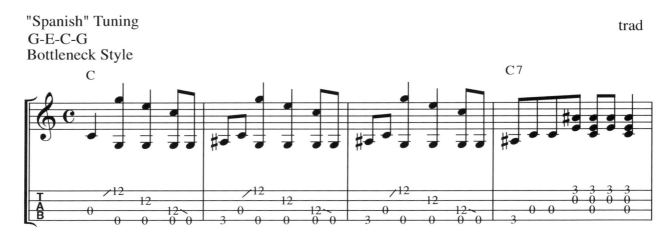

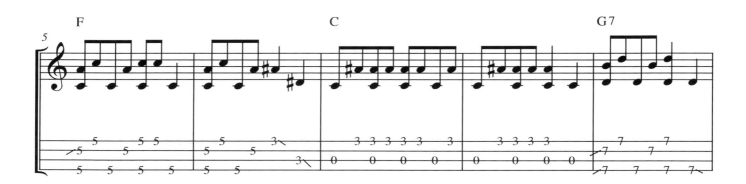

46

"Tell Me Baby" is a 12 bar blues I made up to get students started playing bottleneck slide uke.

Retune to "Spanish" tuning by dropping the A string a whole tone to G.

Measures 1 - 3: Starting somewhere around the 9th or 10th fret, slide up to the 12th fret. Don't forget to damp the notes behind the slide. Be careful with the 8th notes in the bass–they work as a "kicker" to set up the next phrase.

Measure 4: Fret the notes on the top string using one of your fingers behind the slide.

Measures 5 & 6: Use the slide as a full barre at fret 5. Take your time with the two falls at the end of measure 6.

Measures 7 & 8: Same as measure 4.

Measure 11: Here's a typical blues turnaround, similar to the playing of Robert Johnson. Since I place the bottleneck on my pinky, I use the three remaining fingers on my left hand to fret the bass string, and my right hand thumb, ring and middle fingers to pick the strings.

Tell Me, Baby

Tell me, baby, where did you sleep last night?
Came home this morning, the sun was shining bright
Tell me baby, where'd you sleep last night?
Came home this morning, your clothes don't fit you right

Listen to me, baby, what I say is true
You can't love me and love another man, too
Listen to me, baby, everything I say is true
You can't love me and love another man, too

I woke up this morning, I could tell something's wrong,
It looked like my baby had packed her things and gone
I woke up this morning, I could tell something's wrong
It looked like my baby had packed up and gone

Guitar Rag

From Sylvester Weaver

trad

'Vastopol Tuning
G-B-D-G

Bottleneck style

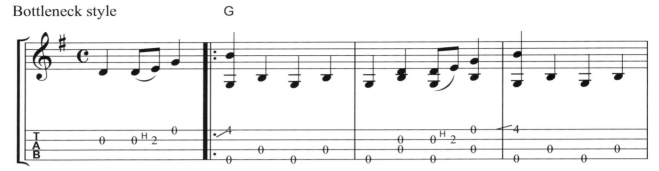

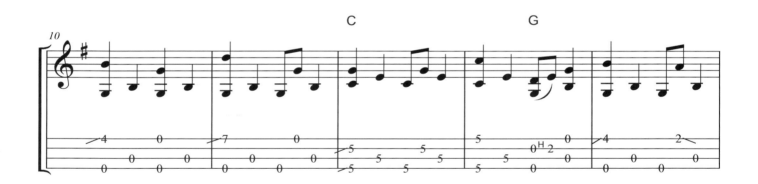

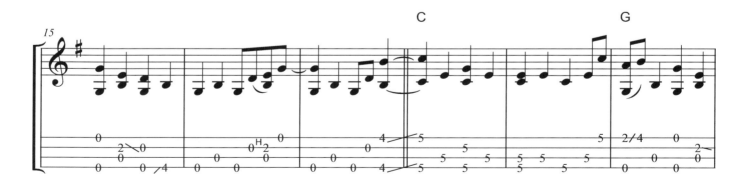

48

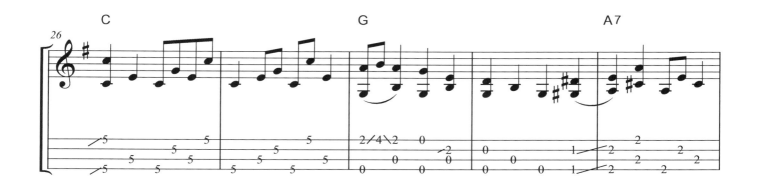

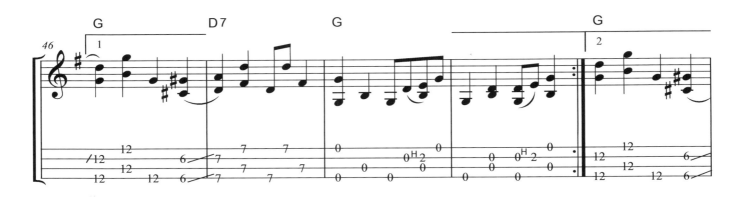

Sylvester Weaver—credited with being the first blues guitarist on record—was the inspiration for one of the biggest Country and Western hits of all time.

In 1923, Weaver backed singer Sara Martin, a popular vaudeville star of the day, on two sides. His fingerpicked accompaniment was the first time *any* blues guitarist had been recorded.

A little over one week later, he recorded the first blues instrumentals, "Guitar Blues" and a snappy slide number called "Guitar Rag."

In 1927, he reworked the tune, adding a new middle section. In 1936 that recording—retitled "Steel Guitar Rag"—became a huge hit for Western Swing pioneer Bob Wills and his great steel guitarist Leon McAuliffe.

In all likelihood, Weaver originally played his guitar Hawaiian style on his lab with a steel bar rather than a bottleneck slide.

"Guitar Rag" has become a staple for both steel and bottleneck players, so it is only natural to play it on the uke, too.

Retune your uke to 'Vastapol tuning by dropping your first string from A to G. Lower your second string a whole step from E to D; and drop the third string a half step from C to B. The open strings sound a G chord major: G-B-D-G.

You can use many of the same licks you played in "Spanish"—open C—tuning. As in that tuning, the IV chord is played with a barre at the 5th fret and the V at the 7th fret. The biggest difference is the relationship of the first string to the rest of the strings: it is the tonic in open C and the fifth in this tuning.

The song has three parts, each 16 bars long. Repeat it as many times as you like, taking the first ending each time until you want to take it home.

When you get to the second ending, let the tempo slow down just a bit to build up the tension. I usually hold the slide at the 11th fret a little longer than notated, then play a huge long gliss from around the 5th fret all the way up to the 12th.

John Henry
From Etta Baker

trad

'Vastopol Tuning
G-B-D-G

Bottleneck style

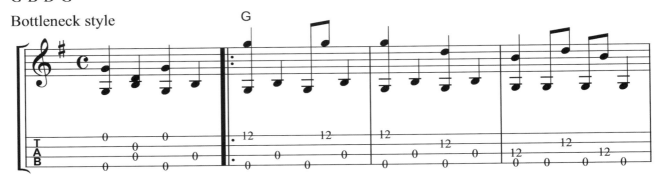

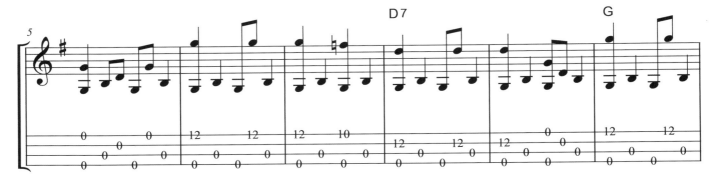

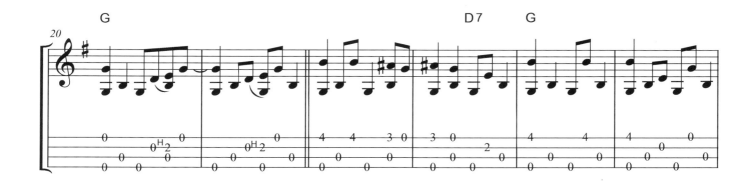

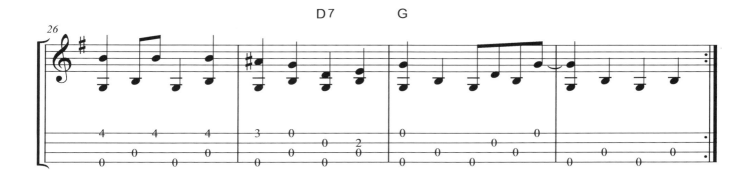

This slide version of the African-American classic ballad is based on the masterful guitar playing of Piedmont blues great Etta Baker.

Although she'd begun playing guitar around 1916 at the tender age of three, her first recording session wasn't until 1956 as part of Paul Clayton's seminal *Instrumental Music from the Southern Appalachians* LP.

As with "Guitar Rag," re-tune your uke to an open G chord: G-B-D-G.

I did not indicate all of the slides in this TAB, so you are on your own. Generally speaking, always slide into a note from some distance below it.

When you see a hammer-on, as in measure 13, use a finger, not the slide.

Don't forget to "fall off" the last note in a phrase by letting the slide move down the fretboard just before the note decays.

"Blues is a natural fact, is something that a fellow lives. If you don't live it you don't have it.
Young people have forgotten to cry the blues. Now they talk and get lawyers and things."
Big Bill Broonzy

Shakin' That Thing

There's a great big mystery
And it sure is worrying me
It's Diddy Wa Diddy
Diddy Wa Diddy
I wish someone would tell me what Diddy Wa Diddy Means

Ragtime, that hugely popular 19th Century piano music popularized by the great African-American composer Scott Joplin, had a bawdier side. They called it *hokum*: rowdy melodies with salacious lyrics performed in juke joints, honky tonks and brothels.

At the dawn of the recording age, jug bands, string bands and soloists adapted ragtime syncopation and chord progressions to their guitars, banjos and ukes. Performers like The Memphis Jug Band, Cannon's Jug Stompers and Blind Blake waxed songs about drinking, dope, sex, and living the wild life. Double–and *single*–entendres were the order of the day–the dirtier, the better.

Of course, no respectable person would be caught dead with one of these records in their house. I wonder who bought all those copies?

Yas Yas Yas

from Blind Blake Alphonso Higgs

trad

Standard tuning

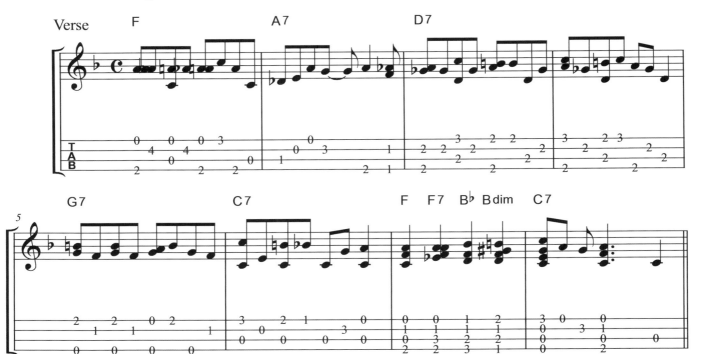

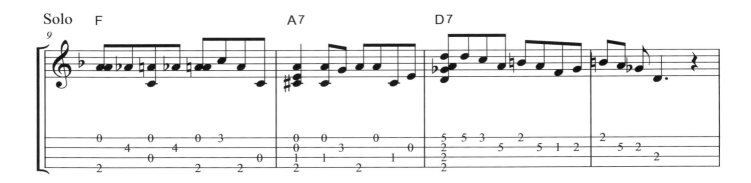

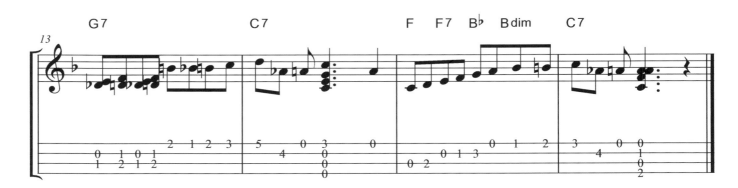

"The Duck's Yas Yas Yas" was originally recorded in St. Louis by pianist James "Stump" Johnson in late 1928. Long a brothel standard, it has been recorded by just about everyone.

In the 1940s and 50s, Bahamian singer Blind Blake Alphonso Higgs–not to be confused with the blues guitarist Blind Arthur Blake–led the swingingest string band in Nassau. Playing tenor banjo, he sang everything from straight-up calypso to ballads, folk songs and novelty numbers.

Blind Blake's version is slightly more presentable than some of the others.

Yas, Yas Yas

Mama bought a rooster, she took it for a duck
She brought him to the table with his two legs up
In came sister with a spoon and a glass
She started spooning up the gravy from his yas yas yas

She bought another rooster, she took it for a hen
She thought it would lay an egg, about nine or ten
She built him a nest with some straw and grass
But he didn't lay nothing but his yas yas yas

Mama, mama, take a look at Sis
She's out in the back yard and she's dancing like this
She said, "Better come in gal, and come here fast
And stop that shakin' your yas yas yas!"

The old folks do it mama but these are modern days
Now the young folks teach the old folks just what to do,
They say, "Shake your shoulders, and shake them fast,
And if you can't shake your shoulders shake your yas yas yas."

Way down yonder in Saint Augustine
A black cat sat on a sewing machine
The sewing machine, it sewed so fast
It sewed ninety-nine stitches in his yas yas yas

Now John Dillinger rode to a gasoline station
He said, "This looks like a pretty good location."
The attendant said, "Would you like some gas?"
He replied, "It's either your gas or your yas yas yas."

The bull frog sat on a mountain peak
And he dipped his tail in a hot pan of grease.
He said, "Excuse me ladies and gentlemen, won't you kindly let me pass?
'Cause I'm slippin', slidin', skiddin' on my yas yas yas."

It was the night before Christmas, everybody was in the house
Not a creature was stirring, not quiet as a mouse
When over by the chimney, I heard something pass,
It was Santa Claus slidin' on his yas yas yas.

Okolehao Blues

from Norman Clark

trad

Low G tuning

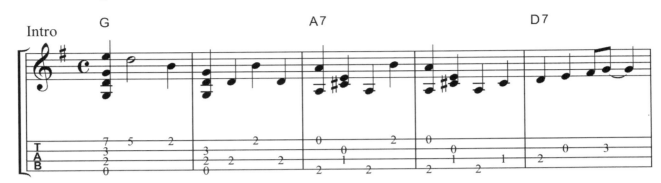

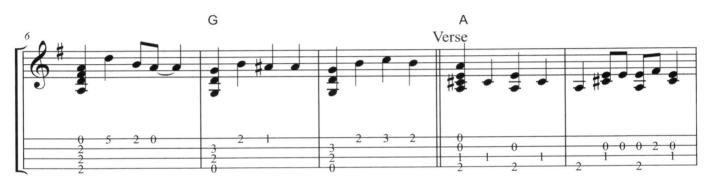

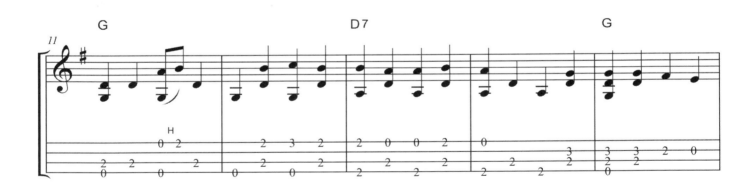

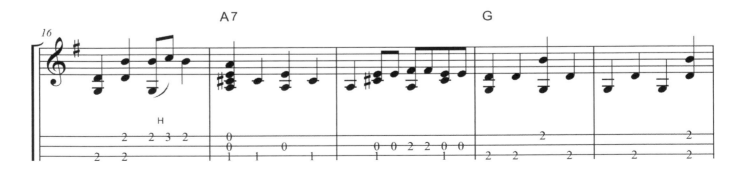

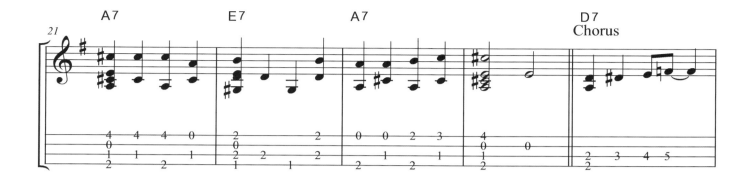

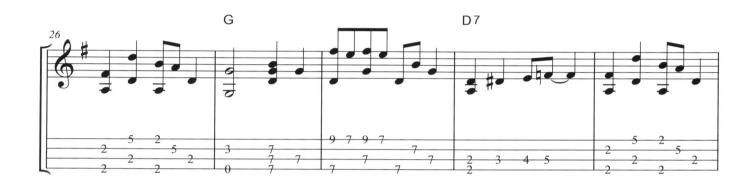

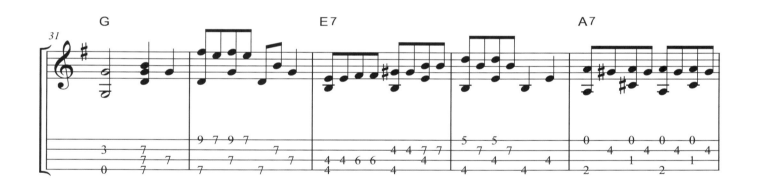

I learned this from homemade mixtape of vintage *hapa-haole* and Hawaiian songs that had passed from fan to fan. Most of the music was familiar to me, but not this odd little number. From the cool Hawaiian guitar introduction to the semi-operatic vocal to the goofy words it just jumped out and grabbed me.

I really don't know much about Norman Clark and His South Sea Islanders other than he recorded for Columbia in the late '20s. To date I have only been able to track down a couple more of his recordings.

Okolehao—which roughly translates as "Iron Butt"—is Hawaiian moonshine. Something to sing about, indeed.

Pronounce it to rhyme with "Go throw hay, cow." Now that's something else to sing about!

Okolehao Blues

In Honolulu, where they do the hula-hula
They've got a drink that can't be beat
That will knock you off your feet
When you start playing, hula girlies start a-swaying
Everybody gathers near, and this is what you'll hear, well:

chorus
Oh I've got those O–Okolehao Blues
Oh those blues I simply can't let loose.
You may rave about your grape juice and your lemonade
But nothing in this world is finer made
Than O–O–O–O–O Okolehao

Blues You Can Use
Blue Notes

What is it that makes the blues *sound* like the blues? One characteristic is the use of blue notes, tones outside of traditional European harmony. Blue notes sound dissonant when played against major chords, adding tension. Or, to put it another way, blue notes sound funky.

Here is a C major scale:

The I, IV and V7 chords built from this scale are C, F and G7. No surprises there.

But add a couple extra tones and you get this:

Those tones—the flatted third and flatted seventh—are the blue notes. Now when you build your I, IV and V chords, you get this:

The V7 is the same—the F note that makes a G chord a G7 already existed in the original major scale—but now you get those bluesy-sounding I7 and V7 chords.

Blue notes work in other ways, too. Play the blues scale against all three chords and you hear a sweet funky dissonance thanks to those blue notes, the Eb and Bb. Why? A C major chord is spelled C-E-G; so the Eb and the E notes clash. Ditto with the IV chord; Bb is a half-step above A, the third of an F triad. Lastly, that Bb is a half step below B, the third of the V chord. In each chord, the other blue note messes with your ears, too. F'rinstance, Eb is the flat seven of F and the flat six of G.

Here's another variation of the blues scale. This one adds a flatted fifth, the notorious "Devil's Interval." Maybe that's why they say that the Devil's got all the good songs.

Sister Maude Mule
from Alec Johnson

trad

Low G tuning

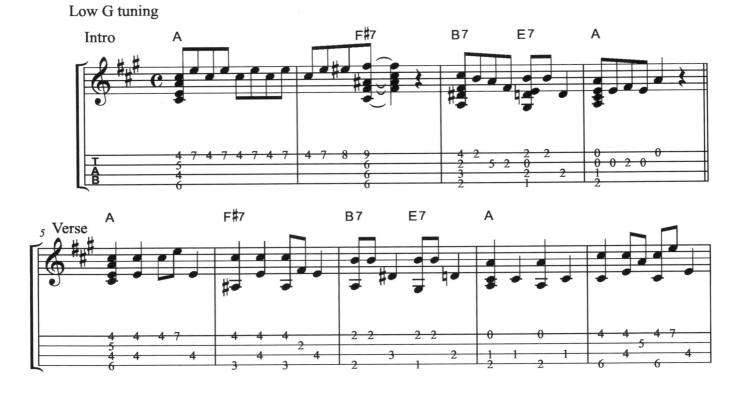

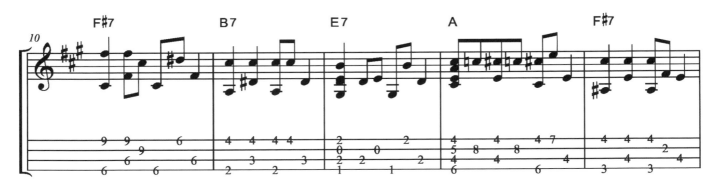

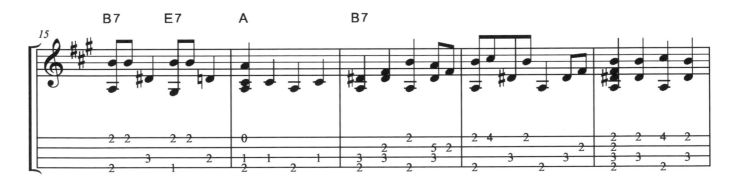

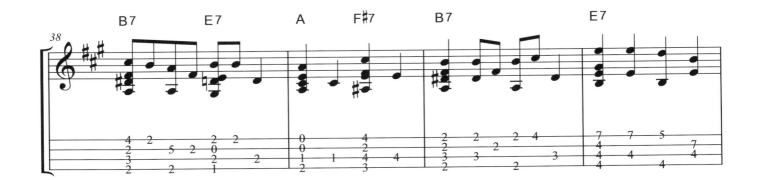

Anyone who has ever spent time with a balky mule will immediately relate to this song from Alec Johnson. Johnson made a number of great recordings in the 20s and 30s, often with Charlie McCoy on mandolin and Bo Carter playing the fiddle.

I generally alternate vocal and instrumental choruses. Be sure to alter the picking and the melody each time; throw in a few extra blue notes, or leave 'em out. Or try some licks based on different chord inversions then the ones I put in the TAB.

Sister Maude Mule

Sister Maude Mule had an awful high temper
She must have been born that way
She kept her papa busy, turnin' down her damper
Cause she was red hot all day,
Before she'd give an inch she'd take a mile, and sometimes she'd take two
There was nothing you would ask of her, but what she'd say to you:

I ain't gonna do it, try to make me do it
You can't make me do it, that's all.
You can hem and haw, kick and paw and argue till you fall,
You can lead a mule to water, you can make him stop
But you can't make the fool drink a doggone drop
I ain't gonna do it, wouldn't attempt do it
I ain't gonna do it, that's all

I ain't gonna do it, said I wouldn't do it
I ain't gonna do it, that's all
You can rave and rant, hew and pant, snort until you ball
You can point your pistol at me, you can call the law,
And I'll fight you till I'm grayer than a rat's grandpa
I ain't gonna do it, swear I wouldn't do it
I ain't gonna do it, that's all

I ain't gonna do it, said I wouldn't do it,
And I won't do it, that's all.
You can rave and rant, hew and pant, snort until you ball,
You can call the whole militia, call the colonel, too
Let 'em put the fireworks on me and see what I'll do.
I ain't gonna do it, said I wouldn't do it,
I won't do it, that's all.

Diddy Wa Diddy #2
from Blind Arthur Blake

trad

Low G tuning

Verse

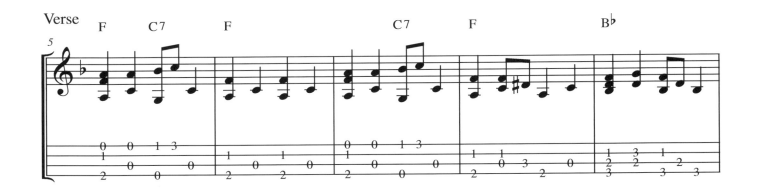

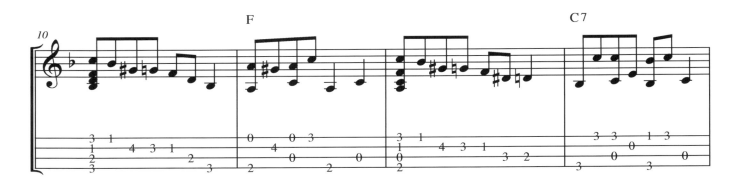

Solo

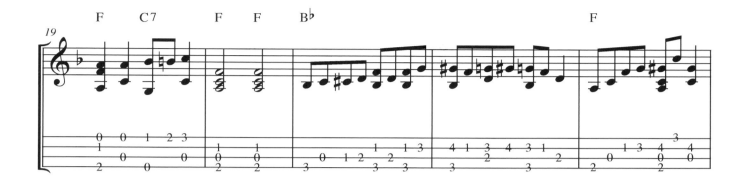

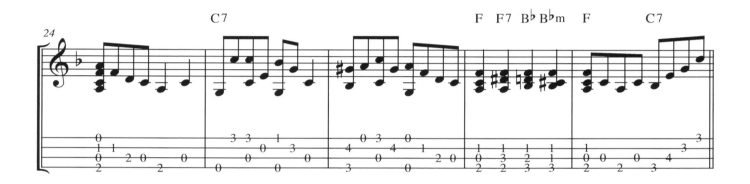

Verse or solo

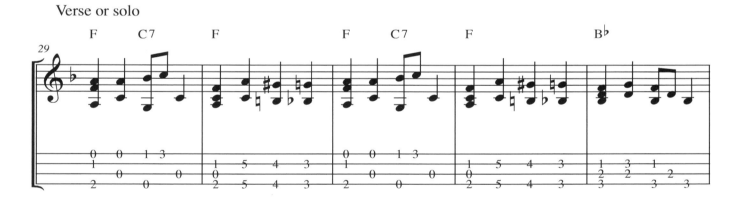

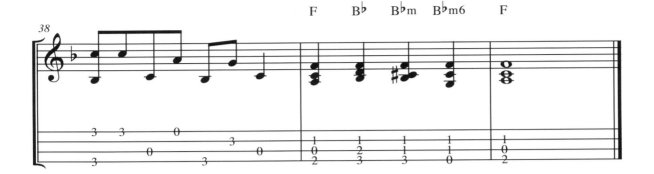

Blind Arthur Blake (1886-1934) was a prodigiously accomplished and influential guitarist. He recorded some 80 sides between 1926 and 1932, revealing a highly complex syncopated ragtime fingerpicking guitar style.

One of his biggest hits—"Diddy Wa Diddy"—asked the eternal question: "I wish somebody would tell me what Diddy Wa Diddy means?"

So he returned to the studio and recorded his own response song: "Diddy Wa Diddy #2," with the refrain "I just found out what Diddy Wa Diddy means."

Both songs share the same melody, chord structure and many of the same guitar licks; not that Blake ever played the same thing twice. He was known for flashy runs, swinging syncopation and bass lines as complicated as a stride pianist's.

In the TAB I give your a small sampling of how I approach the song on the uke. Generally speaking, I try to change the picking with each vocal chorus or instrumental solo. The three parts, then, are best taken as points of departure for your own improvisations.

A gangster shot his pal today
As they carried him away I heard him say
"Diddy Wa Diddy"
He said, "Diddy Wa Diddy
I just found out what Diddy Wa Diddy means."

The police walked right up to him
"Look who's here old two gun Jim,"
Mr. Diddy Wa Diddy
Mr. Diddy Wa Diddy
I just found out what Diddy Wa Diddy means

When they took him to jail he began to shout
The judge says, "That won't get you out,"
Mr. Diddy Wa Diddy etc.

The gangster said, "Now that ain't right,
I caught that guy about my wife,"
My Diddy Wa Diddy, etc.

He told the judge, "Better let me free.
It'll get you some day, you wait and see,"
Mr. Diddy Wa Diddy etc.

The judge says, "Don't give me no sass,
I'm going to lock up your yas, yas, yas,"
Mr. Diddy Wa Diddy etc

"You been around here scaring' folks to death,
I'm going to send you where you can catch your breath,"
Mr. Diddy Wa Diddy" etc

The gangster's wife ran in the door,
Says, "Judge let me get it, just one time more,"
His Diddy Wa Diddy, etc

The judge say, "I'm sorry for you,
His Diddy Wa Diddy days are through"
Mr. Diddy Wa Diddy, etc

"Next time you see your honey cup,
His Diddy Wa Diddy will be dried up."
Mr. Diddy Wa Diddy
He'll need a new Diddy Wa Diddy
I just found out what Diddy Wa Diddy means

"The Blues is Life."
Brownie McGhee

Livin' a Ragtime Life

I've got a ragtime dog and a ragtime cat
A ragtime piano in my ragtime flat
Wear ragtime clothes from hat to shoes
I read a paper called the Ragtime News
Got ragtime habits and I talk that way
I sleep in ragtime and I rag all day
Got ragtime troubles with my ragtime wife
I'm certainly living a ragtime life

Jefferson & Roberts 1906

Born of bawdy-house pianos; melding European harmonies, brass band marches and gut bucket blues; and played with a ragged syncopation, ragtime was at its peak in the early 1900s. Scott Joplin took ragtime out of the brothel and into genteel parlors via compositions like "Maple Leaf Rag," which sold half a million copies by 1909.

Though ragtime's popularity faded with the First World War, it influenced everything from jazz to rural string band music.

The final arrangements look at different approaches to playing ragtime. "Hale's Rag" and "Dill Pickle Rag" both were shaped by Appalachian fiddle bands. "Palakiko Blues" was recorded by a Hawaiian steel guitarist, and "Kona Rag" is my take on a classic blues guitar rag.

Hale's Rag

from Theron Hale and Daughters

trad

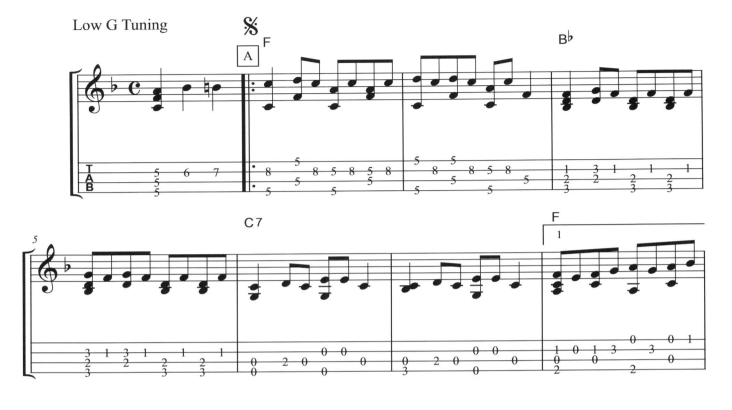

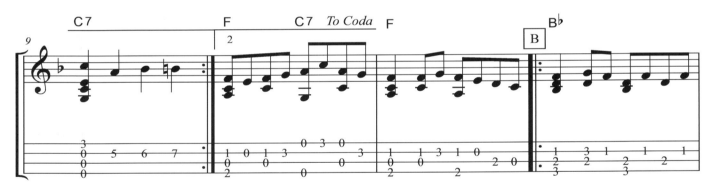

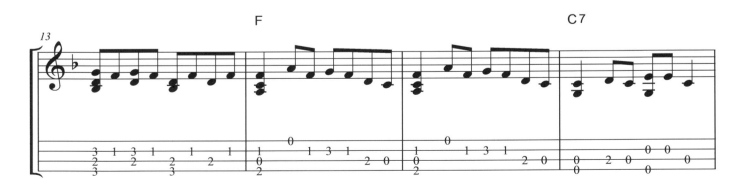

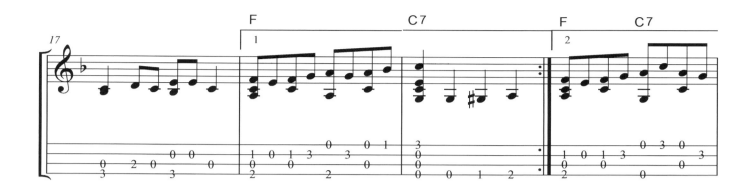

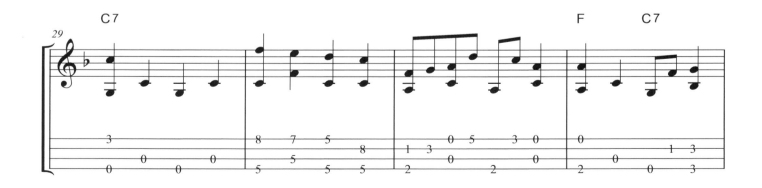

73

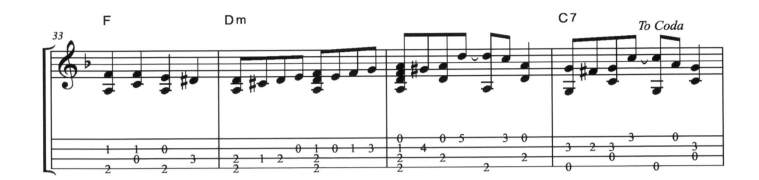

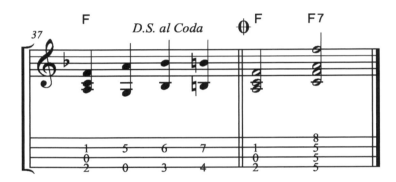

From a wonderful old 78 by the Tennessee fiddle band "Theron Hale and Daughters." Mr. Hale was a featured fiddler with the Grand Old Opry for many years.

To my knowledge, this is the first time it has been attempted on the uke.

"Hale's" follows a typical three part ragtime form; you'll see it again in "Dill Pickle Rag" and "Palakiko Blues." Often, as here, you play all the way through the form once or twice, ending after the first section.

I was surprised at how easily "Hale's Rag" fits on the uke; it just falls right out of the chord positions. About the only alteration I had to make was in the B section, where I took a couple of measures down an octave to avoid an impossibly long jump up the neck.

Play it at a medium tempo, and don't forget to make it swing.

Dill Pickle Rag

Charles L. Johnson

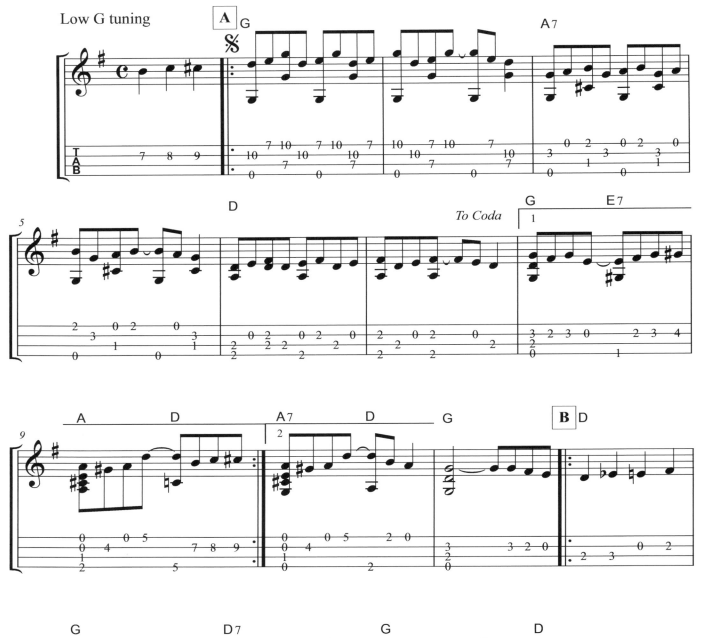

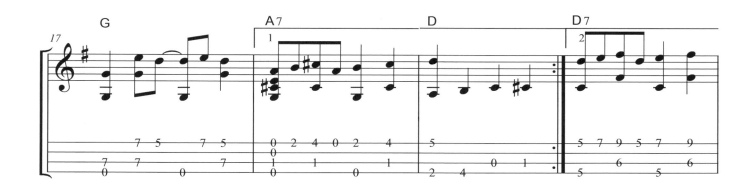

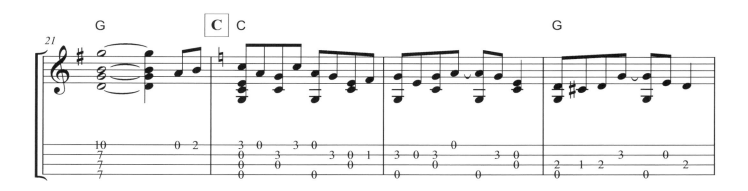

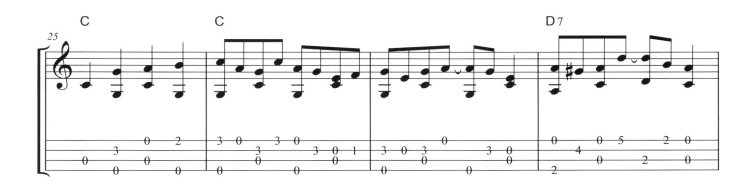

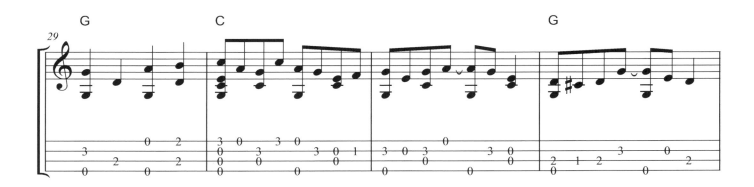

77

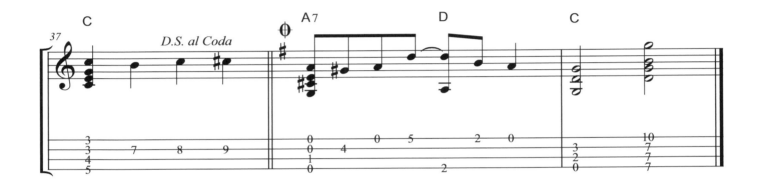

Charles Johnson (born 1876 in Kansas City, Kansas, died 1950 in Kansas City, Missouri) was a prolific composer, with some 300 published songs to his credit. "Dill Pickles," published in 1906, became the second rag to sell one million copies. The first? Scott Joplin's "Maple Leaf Rag."

"Dill Pickle Rag" found new life as a string band tune long after the ragtime era had waned. Nowadays it is much better known as a Bluegrass picker's showpiece.

The "three-against-four" picking pattern in the A section might take a little getting used to.

Measures 2 & 3: Hold a partial barre at the 7th fret for the G chord. I use my ring finger for the 10th fret, second string and my pinky for the jump up to the 10th fret, first string.

Measure 9: Quickly jump to a D7 chord barred at the 5th fret just before beat three.

The B and C sections shouldn't give you any trouble.

Palakiko Blues

from Frank Ferera

trad

Low G tuning

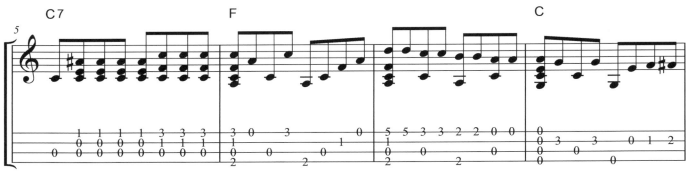

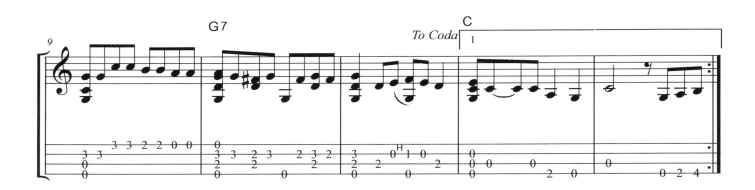

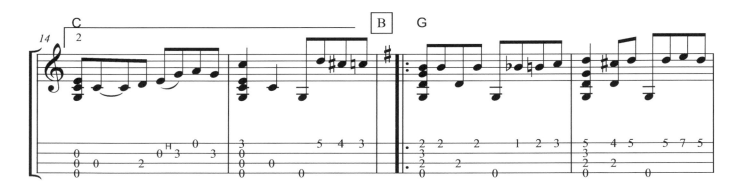

81

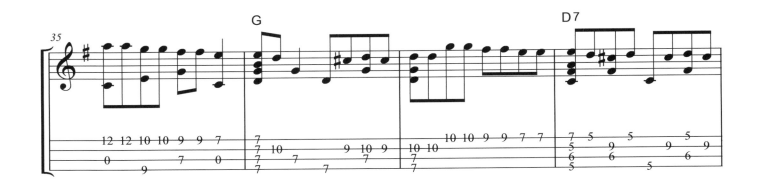

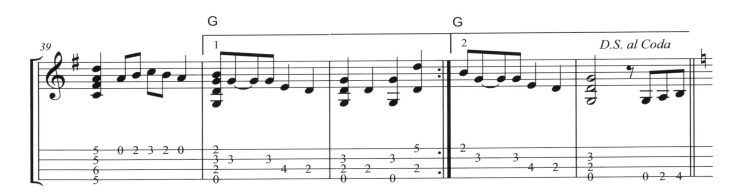

Although originally recorded by Hawaiian steel guitar pioneer Frank Ferara in 1917, I first heard this played by the great blind fiddler and mandolinist Kenny Hall. He called it "Hawaiian Blues." My uke arrangement combines elements of both the steel guitar and the mandolin versions.

Frank Ferara was born in Hawaii and quickly became a master of the newly invented steel guitar. He was a popular recording artist–one of the first Hawaiian musicians to gain worldwide fame. "Palakiko"–the Hawaiian pronunciation of the name "Francis"–was most likely written by Ferara.

The piece has an unusual structure. The A section is a 12 bar blues, the second part is only 8 bars long, and the C section rambles on for a full 16 bars.

Measures 1 - 12: Much of the A section is played out of first position chords, with single notes and double stops thrown in for good measure. Where possible, strive for a languid, legato feel appropriate to Island music.

Things start to get tricky in the B section.

Measures 16 & 17: Most of this is played while holding down a G chord, but you may have to let go for some of the single note runs.

Measures 18 & 19: Nothing like a jump from first position to a barre on the 9th fret in the space of a single eighth note to wake you up! It took me about a week to get it, so take your time.

Measures 20 & 21: Basically, you are bouncing between a couple of inversions of a D7 chord, with some single note stuff thrown in to keep it interesting.

Measure 26: Back to the lower end of the fretboard and smooth sailing. At least for a while.

Measures 33 & 34: Use the double stops to walk up the neck. Immediately after the double stop at the 7th fret, switch fingers on the 4th string to play the note at the 9th fret. That will set you up for the descending run in the next measure.

Measures 36 & 37: Hold a barre at the 7th fret for both measures.

Measures 38 & 39: Most of this is played out of a D7 chord barred at the 5th fret. I use my pinky to reach up to the note on the 9th fret, 2nd string. After playing the chord in measure 39; let everything go and play the open first string. This gives you the time to get back down the neck to set up the last few measures.

After repeating the C section with the second ending, go back to the top and play the A section again, then jump to the coda.

Kona Rag

Mark Nelson

Low G Tuning

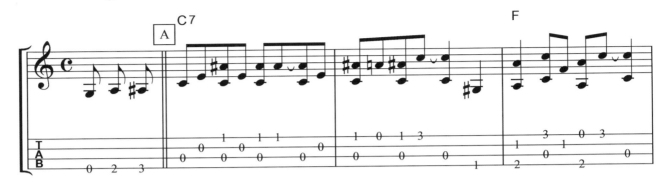

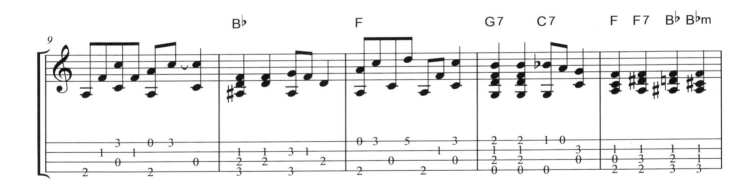

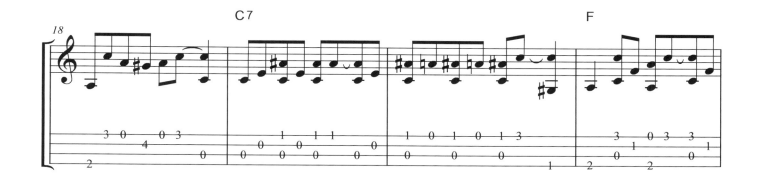

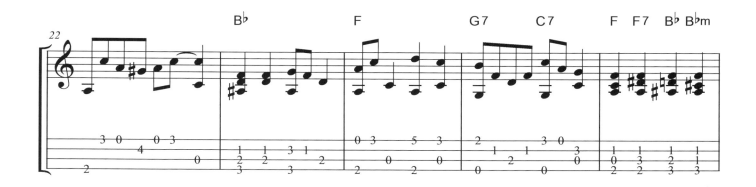

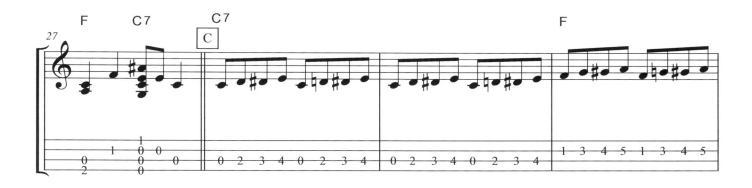

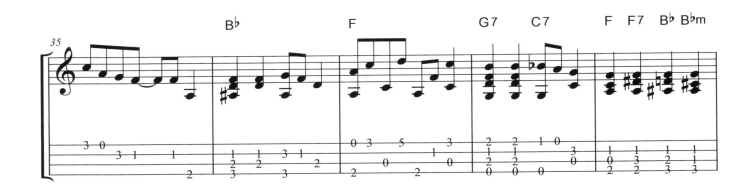

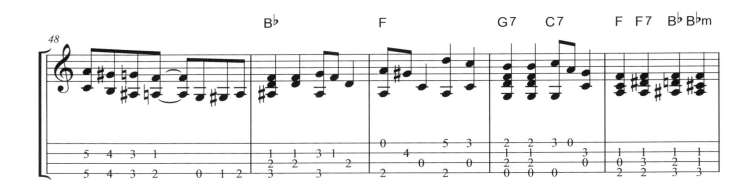

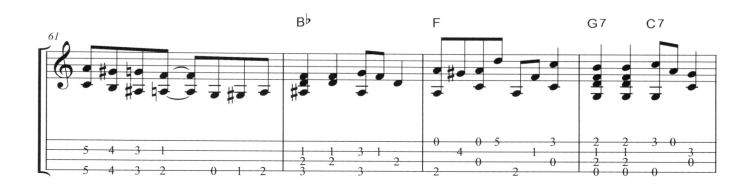

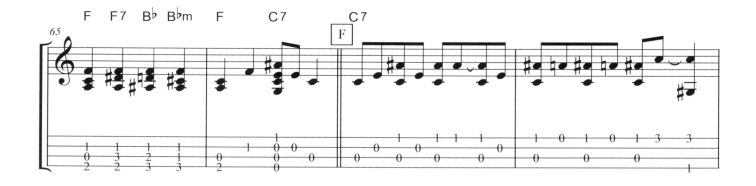

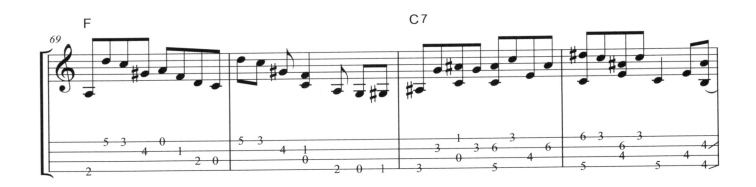

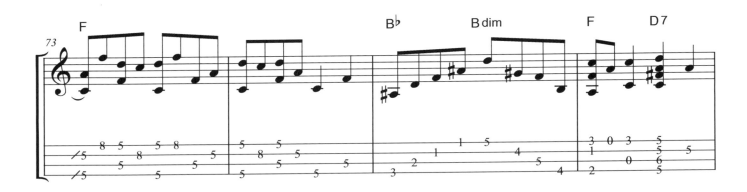

I wrote this a few years back to give my uke students something to chew on. It is loosely based on a Big Bill Broonzy guitar improvisation.

"Kona Rag" is typical type of string band rag. It features a short, repetitive chord progression over which the player spins an ever-evolving web of variations. Often these tunes have no set structure save that you return to the main theme every so often.

For "Kona Rag" the first 13 bars–yes, it is a 13 bar blues–serve as the thematic ground for everything that follows. I've labeled each section, but I do not necessarily play them in the order given here. For instance, I might play the A section twice before moving on to B and C. Then I'll go back and play A again, skip forward to D, and play through to the end.

Of course, nothing written here is sacrosanct–I never play anything the same way twice, and you shouldn't either. So take these variations as the ground upon which to build your own arrangement.

That's what juke'n the uke is all about.

"Simple music is the hardest to play, and the blues is simple music."
Albert Collins

Blues You Can Use
Chord Inversions

Many of the arrangements in this book make use of these chords up the neck.

Major triads

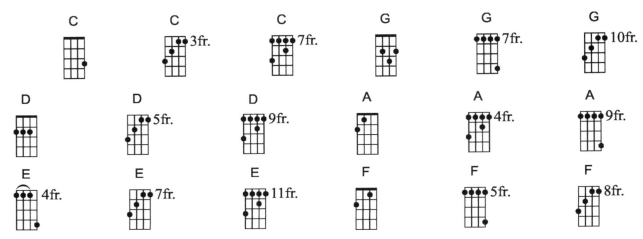

Dominant 7ths

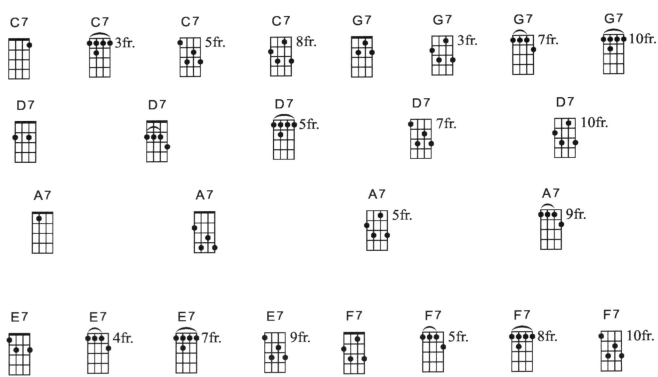

Minor triads

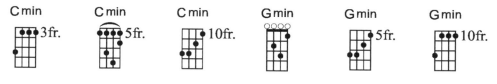

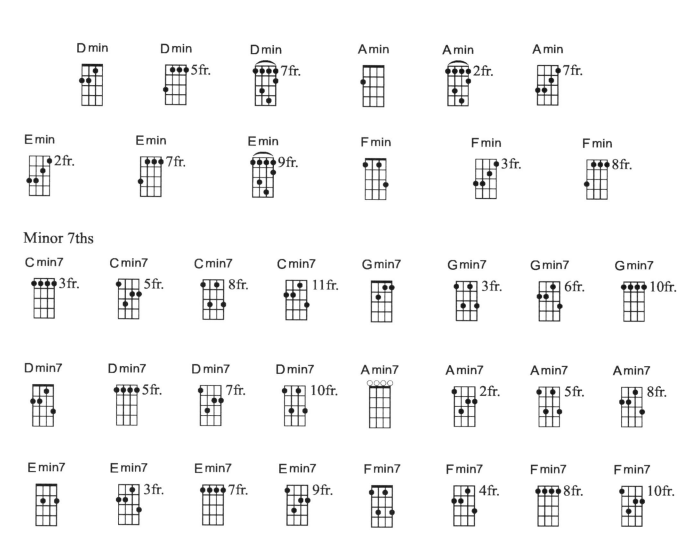

Minor 7ths

An ability to quickly transpose to a new key on the fly is one of the most valuable skills a musician can learn. Fortunately, it is also one of the easiest.

I touched on the subject in the lesson on page 30. The trick is to think of a set of chords in terms of their relation to each other and to the key of the song.

Remember the I, IV and V chords in a 12 bar blues? Each chord is built upon—and takes it's name from—one of the notes of the major scale. Counting up the notes of a C major scale, you get this:

C	D	E	F	G	A	B	C
1	2	3	4	5	6	7	8

So in the key of C, the I chord is built on C, the first note of the scale; the IV on F, the fourth note, and the V chord would be G. This holds no matter what key you are in; here's a Bb major scale:

Bb	C	D	Eb	F	G	A	Bb
1	2	3	4	5	6	7	8

Your I, IV and V chords will be Bb, Eb and F. Don't worry about flats and/or sharps right now, they pretty much take care of themselves. The next step is to work backwards from an existing chord progression.

What is going on with this typical ragtime chord progression?

C	A7	D7	G7

Looking at the first chart above, we can use numbers for each chord, like this:

C	A7	D7	G7
1	6	2	5

Or, in Roman numerals: I-VI-II-V

Transposed to Bb, the progression becomes:

Bb	G7	C7	F7
I	VI	II	V

This works for minor chords, too. Here's another typical chord progression. Note that this one ends on the tonic chord:

Dm7	Gm7	Cm7	F7	Bb6

Here's how the chords relate to the key center, Bb. We use lower case numerals for minor chords, but the principle's the same:

Dm7	Gm7	Cm7	F7	Bb6
iii	vi	ii	V	I

Transposed back to C we get this:

Em7	Am7	Dm7	G7	C6
iii	vi	ii	V	I

And that's all there is to it! A little effort working out the chordal relationships for each song in this book and then transposing to a different key would be time well spent.

Sure, there is more to learn—like, what the heck is a minor 7 flat 5 chord?—but that is a question for another day. Be sure to check out my website for more music theory lessons. A little knowledge is a good thing.

Blues You Can Use
Transposing Chart for Baritone Ukes

All of the songs in this book may be played on baritone ukes with a minimum of fuss. Just play the TAB as written and ignore the chord names; all of the fingerings will work just fine. Of course, because the baritone is tuned a fourth lower that the smaller ukes, you will be in a different key.

So how do you know what chords you *are* playing? You have a couple of choices. The best is to follow through with the lesson on the previous page. Figure out the numerical relationships for each chord progression, and then transpose down a fourth (or up a fifth, it comes out the same).

Here's a handy chart. The top row is the original chord as written for the uke, the bottom row is what that same chord shape becomes on the baritone uke.

C	C#/Db	D	D#/Eb	E	F	F#/Gb	G	G#/Ab	A	A#/Bb	B
G	G#/Ab	A	A#/Bb	B	C	C#/Db	D	D#/Eb	E	F	F#

Juke'n The Uke
Blues, Ragtime & Hokum for 'Ukulele
CD Program

That Lonesome Train That Took My Baby Away
Fishin' Blues
Hale's Rag
K.C. Moan Blues
Diddy Wa Diddy #2
Staggerlee
Wild Cow Blues
Yas Yas Yas
Okolehao Blues
Sister Maude Mule
John Henry
Let the Mermaids Flirt With Me
Palakiko Blues
Blues in the Bottle
Kona Rag

Pick up your copy today! There is no better way to learn this music. It's a rockin' little record, if I say so myself.

Available at **www.mark-o.com** and many other fine online retailers.

You can find audio and/or video files for "Hey Hey," "Richland Woman Blues," "Guitar Rag," "Tell Me Baby." "Movin' Day" and "Dill Pickle Rag" on my website, too.

Mark Kailana Nelson

Multi-instrumentalist Mark Nelson has carved a unique niche for himself as an entertainer, musician and educator. His deep love and understanding of traditional music led him to the mastery of several different musical idioms, ranging from blues to old time music, Celtic to Hawaiian. In a career that began well before he was able to drive, he has performed everywhere from street corners and hay barns to festivals and the concert stage in the US, Europe and Canada. He once worked as a banjo playing gorilla in Dublin, but that's a different story.

Mark lives in Southern Oregon's Applegate Valley with his wife Annie and various furred and finned friends, where he divides his time between studio work, writing, and watching the trees grow.

Selected Discography

Slack Key Style 'Ukulele
Funtime Uke-A-Rama
Ke Kukima Polinahe
Old Time Hawaiian Slack Key Guitar
The Water is Wide
autumn…
The Faery Hills
After the Morning
The Rights of Man

Books

Learn to Play Slack Key Style 'Ukulele
Learn to Play Fingerstyle Solos for 'Ukulele
Old Time Hawaiian Slack Key Guitar
Learn to Play Hawaiian Slack Key Guitar
Ke Kukima Polinahe: Hawaiian Music For Dulcimer
Favorite Old Time American Songs for Appalachian Dulcimer
The Complete Collection of Celtic Music for Appalachian Dulcimer
Fiddle Tunes for Dulcimer: The Rights of Man

Mark Nelson
Acme Arts
PO Box 967
Jacksonville, OR 97530
www.Mark-o.com

Audio and/or video files the songs in this book are available for download at www.Mark-o.com

Mark is proud to endorse **Po Mahina 'Ukulele and Guitars**, made by Big Island luthier Dennis Lake.
PO Box 845
Na'alehu, HI 96772
www.Konaweb.com/Mahina

Mark also endorses the great resonator ukes made by **Mya-Moe 'Ukulele**.
18 Forbes Road, White Salmon, WA 98672
www.MyaMoeUkulele.com

Made in the USA
Middletown, DE
06 February 2015